Table of Contents

Teacher Information

Teacher How-To's

Teacher Worksheets

Table of Contents

Student Worksheets

Appendices

Introduction to the Internet

Look for these icons to guide you through the book:

Hands On
Refers you to teacher and student worksheets for specific Internet skills practice.

Helpful Hint
Points out experience-based tips, ideas, and suggestions.

Caution!
Highlights important legal, technical, or procedural information.

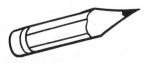

Teacher Worksheet
Included on all teacher worksheets so they are easy to locate.

In your classroom, the Internet can be an effective teaching and learning tool. There is a wealth of information out there for teachers and students to use. The challenge is finding the time and resources to narrow that information and find web sites that are right for your classroom needs. This book can help you do just that.

In the late 1980s, we as teachers became our school's technology "experts." We tried out some projects using a computer hooked to a modem, and spent hours visiting fascinating web sites. It was easy to see how an adult with patience and time for trial and error could get drawn into using the Internet. However, as we began to design exercises and activities for our classrooms, we quickly realized that tailoring the Internet to students is a far more difficult task. Web sites used in the classroom must be age- and subject-matter appropriate, load quickly, link logically to other sites, and, ideally, have interesting graphics. We faced the daunting task of creating an engaging and workable Internet curriculum while maintaining a safe, controlled, classroom environment.

Gradually, we discovered that many search engines have built-in filters which allow only kid-friendly web sites to appear. The road to follow revealed itself to us! We could take students to a kid-safe search engine, give them a little guidance, and watch them surf creatively and learn how to navigate the Internet without stumbling into inappropriate web sites. We planned a strategy for bringing the Internet into our classrooms, including processes for defining and teaching computer skills in a logical order, implementing Internet safety regulations, and arranging our classrooms so that we could keep a watchful eye on our young surfers. In a short time, students had the tools and know-how to find information on the Internet efficiently and safely. They were in control—and so were we!

Our purpose in writing this book is to provide an informative, easy-to-use guide for teachers to introduce their students to the Internet quickly and painlessly, eliminating all the trial and error that we experienced. With this book in hand, your students will discover the electronic world at their fingertips.

What is the Internet?

The Internet grew out of military research efforts to communicate and exchange data instantaneously. Refined in the last decade by the educational community and fed by recent commercial efforts, the Internet now affects the way people across the world send and receive information. Today, people use the Internet for everything from planning a family vacation to researching a family tree.

To understand the Internet, you first need to understand what a **network** is. **A network is a group of computers linked together electronically. The Internet is a giant collection of interacting computer networks.** Perhaps the easiest way to view the Internet is as a huge library that can be referenced from a personal computer. Understanding bookmarking, hyperlinks, and keyword searches will help you and your students navigate this strange new electronic library.

The first part of this book will guide you through the processes of understanding and navigating the Internet, and setting up the guidelines that will safeguard your students' journey into cyberspace. Practice worksheets for you, the teacher, will give you a chance to hone your own Internet skills and prepare activities for your classroom. The second part of this book includes teacher-researched, Internet-based activities designed to help students learn how to become independent Internet surfers. We highly recommend that teachers become familiar with and, if time permits, complete the student worksheets before assigning them to students. This is the best way to familiarize yourself with the assignments, while getting Internet practice along the way.

The Internet can make any place accessible to teachers and students. Proficient Internet users can find and share information about almost any place in the world, even outer space! They can research specific areas of interest, from arts and entertainment to sports and sciences. They can obtain up-to-the-minute news or research ancient civilizations. With appropriate resources and careful planning, the Internet can be an invaluable resource for every classroom teacher.

4 **What is the Internet?**

Be There—Be Aware

Students should always be supervised when using the Internet. The best policy to follow is: **Be There—Be Aware.** Enforce this policy through a combination of good communication and supervision. When considering classroom safety and the Internet, a good first step is to establish an **Acceptable Use Policy** (AUP), a contract providing teachers, parents, and students with a clear set of guidelines defining Internet use and conduct in the classroom. If your school does not already have an AUP, you may want to create one. When creating an AUP, consult media specialists, other teachers, administrators, and parents. Consider legal, copyright, and privacy issues; define expectations for students and teachers. Familiarize yourself with the guidelines you agree upon and communicate them clearly to everyone involved.

To supplement the AUP, discuss with your students why Internet safety is important. Use the **Internet Safety Policy** (page 57) as a basis for this discussion. Use the **Our Classroom Promise** sheet (page 58) to create a set of guidelines that will give your students a feeling of ownership and responsibility. Like the AUP, tailor these safety guidelines to your situation—your students, your classroom, your school system's policies. Include consequences for breaking the promise. Post the promise beside each computer.

It is also important to communicate with parents. Send home the AUP, the Classroom Promise, and the Internet Safety Policy guidelines. Make sure to get a parental signature on the parent portion of the **Internet Safety Policy** (page 57) before letting a student use the Internet, and keep the permission forms on file. We suggest that even young students sign the permission form, so they are a part of the process, too. An increasing number of parents have Internet access at home, and they may enjoy visiting the web sites their children have seen at school. To keep parents involved, use the **Places We Have Been!** form (page 59) to let parents know what your class has been doing, and encourage them to let you know about any web sites they think your class would enjoy.

Finally, give careful consideration to how you place your classroom computer or computers. If you have a good, clear view of all of the computer screens in your classroom, enterprising students will be less inclined to download games or explore web sites unrelated to your classroom activities. Arrange your classroom so you can "monitor" students' progress, spot students who get off track, and guide them back in the right direction.

Helpful Hint

Log on to **www.att.com/edresources/accept.html** to see how other schools are developing AUP's. Also, check with your Internet service provider to see if it can provide parental controls software, which will filter out web sites with adult content. Filtering software can also be purchased online or at a local software dealer, and installed to filter information.

The Bare Net-cessities

There are four essential things you need to be able to "surf the Net." **For further explanation of this or any other terminology, please refer to the Glossary (pages 61-63).**

- **A computer**
- **A modem to connect you to the Internet.** Modems act as interpreters, translating computer language to a form transmittable over phone lines. Some computers have built-in modems, while others require that you purchase an external modem. If you are on a computer network, you do not need a modem.
- **An Internet Service Provider (ISP)**—companies like your local phone or cable company, America OnLine, CompuServe, Prodigy, and Mindspring, that allow you access to the Internet. Some schools serve as their own ISP and have a direct connection to the Internet.
- **Browser software** such as Netscape Navigator or Internet Explorer, usually provided through your ISP.

How to be a Speed Demon

There are many educational and mechanical things you can do to increase your speed and productivity on the Internet. To learn more about the Internet, befriend any resident "experts" at your school. Inquire about in-service training and workshops on Internet use. Best of all, complete the teacher and student worksheets in this book. Practice may not make you perfect, but it will certainly increase your comfort level! On the mechanical side, no one enjoys sitting in front of a computer screen and waiting, waiting, waiting, for a web page to appear. Outdated machinery just can't do the job quickly enough.

To connect to the Internet quickly, you should have the following equipment:

- **A fairly new computer—oldies are not goodies!**
- **A fast (at least 56K) modem—faster <u>is</u> better!**
- **At least 16MB of RAM**

Helpful Hint

Text loads more quickly than graphics. To prevent graphics from loading on a web page, turn off the automatic image loading option (usually under Preferences). Your screen won't be as pretty, but it will load and print more quickly!

Helpful Hint

Quit out of other software before logging on to the Internet.

Logging On

Once your equipment is set up, it is time to log on to the Internet. If your school is on a network, you may not need to go through a log on process; you should be able to click on your browser icon and start surfing. However, many schools require you to log on with a user name and password.

Your user name is your Internet "identity." It can be plain (JaneDoe) or glamorous (Superstar2000). Make it something you can remember—you will have to enter it each time you log on to the Internet. You will also need to choose a **password**. To log on, enter your user name and then your password. The computer will verify your identity and password. If everything is in order, you are granted access to the Internet!

Caution!

Keep your password a secret! Anyone who has access to your password can log on as you, and the computer will not know the difference. Passwords should be at least five characters long, and be a combination of letters and numbers. Choose a password you can remember, but others will not easily guess. Names of pets or family members are not the most secure choices. Also, avoid your school's initials, your middle name, or date of birth.

User Name:	jsmith
Password:	

Change Password...   Cancel   Connect

Your log on screen may look something like this.

Helpful Hint

If your first attempt to log on does not work, check the following: Is everything spelled correctly? Is the modem on? Are all computer and modem cables securely attached? Reenter your user name and password to try again.

Helpful Hint

In your classroom, only you or a designated adult should log on to the Internet. Discuss the importance of keeping passwords secret, even with younger students. **Do not share your teacher password with students.** Although most students are too young to try and hack into someone else's e-mail and files, it is better to be safe than sorry.

Helpful Hint

The first time you use any browser like America Online or Netscape Navigator, the program will guide you through the setup process. It will tell you how to enter a local telephone number and assist you in creating a user name and password. Call the browser's toll free help number if you have problems.

Now I'm There—What Do I Do?

The first screen you see after you sign on is called your **Home Page**. Look at the top of the Home Page. The icons you see are called **buttons**. The row of buttons you see is called the **tool bar**. Below are sample tool bars from Microsoft Internet Explorer and Netscape Navigator.

Microsoft Internet Explorer Tool Bar

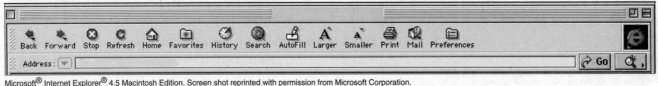

Microsoft® Internet Explorer® 4.5 Macintosh Edition. Screen shot reprinted with permission from Microsoft Corporation.

Netscape Navigator Tool Bar

Netscape Communicator browser window © 1999 Netscape Communications Corporation. Used with permission.

Both of these tool bars appear as they would on a Macintosh computer. Tool bars for an IBM compatible look slightly different, but the buttons shown below are very similar.

Helpful Hint

Tool bars guide you through the Internet in a logical fashion. The icons you see below which appear across the tool bar are called buttons. Some of the most frequently-used buttons are:

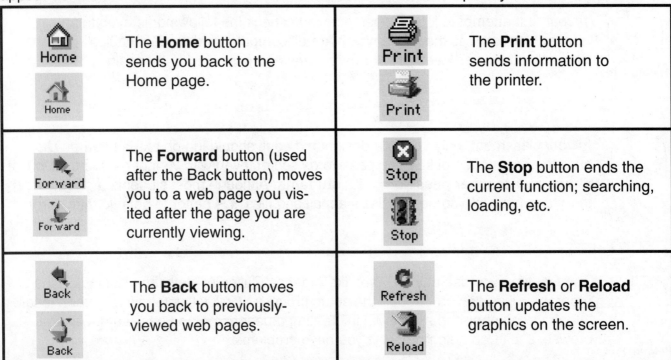

Home / Home	The **Home** button sends you back to the Home page.	Print / Print	The **Print** button sends information to the printer.
Forward / Forward	The **Forward** button (used after the Back button) moves you to a web page you visited after the page you are currently viewing.	Stop / Stop	The **Stop** button ends the current function; searching, loading, etc.
Back / Back	The **Back** button moves you back to previously-viewed web pages.	Refresh / Reload	The **Refresh** or **Reload** button updates the graphics on the screen.

Netscape Communicator browser window © 1999 Netscape Communications Corporation. Used with permission.
Microsoft® Internet Explorer® 4.5 Macintosh Edition. Screen shot reprinted with permission from Microsoft Corporation.

What in the wURLd is a URL?

Each web site has a specific address, like a mailing address, called a **URL (Uniform Resource Locator)**. If you know the URL of a web site, you can type it in, press the Return/Enter key, and go directly to that web site. URLs look something like this:

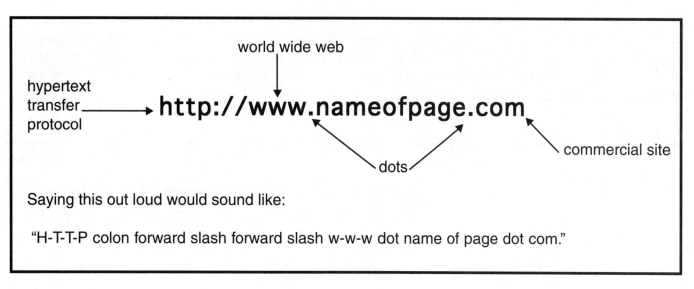

Saying this out loud would sound like:

"H-T-T-P colon forward slash forward slash w-w-w dot name of page dot com."

The abbreviation **"http"** stands for **hypertext transfer protocol,** the language that the Internet uses to communicate. Notice there are never any spaces in URLs. Some URLs are long and have symbols like ~ or _ in them. **The different endings of URLs are called domains**, and can tell you something about the nature of that web site. As new web sites continue to crowd the Internet, watch for more specific domains to appear.

Here are some domain references to help you decipher URLs:

.com	Commercial web site or business address used by a company
.edu	Educational web site, a college, university, or other school
.int	International organizations, such as the Red Cross
.gov	Government agency
.mil	United States military
.net	Network resources
.org	Nonprofit agency or other organization

Some domain names indicate the web site's country of origin, for example:

.au	Australia
.br	Brazil
.ca	Canada
.cn	China
.de	Germany
.fi	Finland
.fr	France
.hk	Hong Kong
.jp	Japan
.uk	United Kingdom

Search Engines

Search Engines sift through the huge amount of information on the Internet and direct you to web sites related to topics of your choosing. Some of the most popular are: Yahoo!, Lycos, Infoseek, AltaVista, Snap, and Excite.

Some search engines are designed specifically for kids. AOL, Classroom Connect, Lycos, and Yahoo! all have kid-safe, filtered search engines. Because we have successfully used Yahoo!'s kid web site, *Yahooligans!* to teach the Internet in our classrooms, the worksheets in this book were developed with *Yahooligans!* as their starting point. With modifications, however, the worksheets can be completed using any search engine.

A Short List of Search Engines for Children
Classroom Connect	www.classroomconnect.com
Lycos Zone	www.lycoszone.lycos.com
Yahooligans!	www.yahooligans.com

A Short List of Search Engines for Adults
AltaVista	http://www.altavista.com
Excite	http://www.excite.com
Infoseek	http://www.infoseek.com
Lycos	http://www.lycos.com
Snap	http://www.snap.com
Yahoo!	http://www.yahoo.com

Caution!

Do not let students use search engines unattended.

Helpful Hint

Set your computer so *Yahooligans!* or the kids' search engine of your choice is your home page. To do this, check the search engine home page. Most search engines have an on-screen command you can click to make it your home page. If not, choose Preferences under the Edit menu, go to Home or Search, and type in your preferred search engine address.

Hyper Activity

Hyperlinks are an easy way to begin exploring the Internet. **Hyperlinks connect you to other web pages with a click of the mouse.** Move your mouse across the screen. When the arrow changes to a pointing hand, you have found a hyperlink. Links that are words are called **hypertext**. They are usually underlined and in a different color. Links that are pictures are called **hypergraphics**.

Hyperlinks are especially important in a primary classroom. Students who can read can navigate the Internet by clicking hypertext links. Students who are still developing reading skills may need someone to help them find and click hyperlinks.

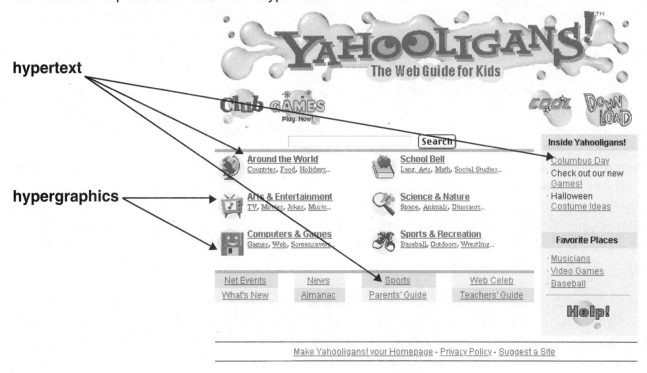

Yahoo! and Yahooligans! are trademarks of Yahoo! Inc.
Copyright © 1994-1999 Yahoo! All Rights Reserved.

Reproduced with the permission of Yahoo! Inc. © 1999 by Yahoo! Inc.
YAHOOLIGANS! and the YAHOOLIGANS! Logo are trademarks of Yahoo! Inc.

Helpful Hint

Let assistant teachers, parent volunteers, or older students help developing readers decipher hyperlinks.

Helpful Hint

If you bring up a web page you do not want to view, use the back arrow (on the menu bar at the top of the page) to return to the previous web page. The computer tracks where you have been and will return to the previous page. You can also click either the Go or History button to backtrack, depending on the browser.

Hands On

Practice using hyperlinks with the Hyperlinks for Teachers worksheet (page 24), and the student hyperlinks worksheets (pages 30-34).

Keys to the Kingdom

Like hyperlinks, using keywords can be helpful when locating information. To start a **keyword search**, look for a box in which to enter your search word. There is usually a Search/Find button beside it. Refer to the example below for a picture of what a Search box may look like.

Suppose you want to find out when migrating whales pass near Hawaii. If you type in the single word *whales* you may get thousands of possible web sites—too many to search! To narrow your search, add additional keywords which will make the search more specific. You can also add additional symbols or certain words, called **qualifiers**, which include or exclude your keywords.

The word *AND* is a useful qualifier. A better way to search for the answer to the whale question above would be to type in *whales AND migrate AND Hawaii*. This will locate only articles that contain all three words. Notice that the word *AND* is capitalized. Using a + sign immediately before a word has the same effect, for example *+whales +migrate +Hawaii*. The word *not* is another qualifier. It excludes words. The search *Washington NOT George NOT district of columbia NOT dc* would exclude articles on George Washington and the District of Columbia, but include Washington state. Similarly, the minus sign is an eliminator. You could enter *+Washington -George -dc* and get similar results. Some search engines let you enclose a phrase in quotation marks, and will search for the exact phrase. If you type in *"whales migrate by Hawaii,"* the engine will search for articles that contain that exact phrase.

Searching with a keyword is a skill that most students can master if they are using a kid-friendly search engine. Students at all reading levels can use keywords with assistance. Most students will need help identifying appropriate keywords, while a few may have the ability to recognize keywords or phrases, but may need help with the actual typing.

Helpful Hint

Following are suggestions for using keywords effectively:
- Be as specific as possible when choosing keywords
- Consider synonyms and alternate spellings of topic words
- Become familiar with your search engine's options and help menu

Hands On

Refer to the teacher worksheet (page 26) and the student worksheets (pages 41-45) to practice using keywords.

Marking Your Spot

Suppose you find a great web page and want to remember where it is. You could write down the URL (remember, that's the http://www.website.com) but it's difficult to type in all of those letters again, and very easy to make a mistake! Fortunately, **you can bookmark special places on the Internet so you can return to them easily.**

To bookmark a page:
- Go to the page you want to bookmark.
- Go to the tool bar at the top of the screen.
- Select Bookmarks or Favorites.
- Slide down to the "add to . . ." option.
- Release the mouse.

To visit a bookmarked web site, go to the tool bar, select **Favorites** or **Bookmark**, slide down to the web site you want to visit, and release the mouse.

To remove a bookmark:
- Select Bookmarks or Favorites.
- Select the name of the web site you want to delete.
- Click the Delete button or press the Delete key on your keyboard. A warning may appear asking if you are sure you want to delete the bookmark.
- If the web site selected is correct, click Yes, OK, or Delete.

Here are some places you may want to mark:
- Search engines you use frequently
- Educational resources sites
- Web sites you will use in classroom activities
- Web sites you visit frequently
- Sites you want your students to visit
- A page with graphics you want to copy

Helpful Hint

Some browsers let you remove a web site from the Favorites or Bookmark menu by dragging the name of the web site directly into the trash (Macs) or recycle bin (PCs) on the desktop.

Helpful Hint

Once you begin using the Internet, you may find that there are many places you want to bookmark. To help you find bookmarks more quickly, you can organize your bookmarks into folders. Check online help directions provided with the Internet software you are using.

Hands On

Use the teacher worksheet (page 25) and the student worksheets (pages 35-40 and 51-54) to bookmark useful web sites.

Some Day My Prints Will Come

The quality of results you get when printing from the Internet depend on how the web page was designed. Sometimes web sites print only one page (usually the page that is visible on your computer screen), while other web sites print multiple pages. Some web sites will print text only, while others will print both text and graphics. It can take a long time to print web pages containing color pictures or complicated backgrounds.

Printing commands are found under the File menu, or you can look for a printer icon on the menu bar. If your computer has a Print Preview option (under the File menu), you can check ahead of time to see what the results will be. Otherwise, you will have to print and see what appears. If you're having trouble printing text directly from the Internet, try copying the text you want and printing it out in a word processing program. Here's how:

To copy text:
- Select the text you want to copy using the "click and drag" method (explained below).
    1. Place the cursor at the beginning of the text.
    2. Hold down the mouse button (this is the "click").
    3. Highlight the desired text by gliding over it (this is the "drag").
    4. Release the mouse.
- Go to the File menu and select Copy.
- Open a document in your word processing program.
- Go to the File menu and select Paste.
- Your text will appear in the new document.

Helpful Hint: Print out web pages that contain colorful graphics and have students use the pictures in a variety of ways. Images can highlight homework folders, collages, mobiles, etc.

Helpful Hint

Hands On: To add web page graphics to classroom worksheets, try the techniques outlined **Grappling with Graphics** (page 16) and **Capture Your Screen** (page 17).

Hands On

Evaluating What You See

This true story shows how using the Internet can help students develop critical thinking skills. A class found a web site about recycling and was taking an online "quiz." One question asked whether it was better to use paper or plastic bags at the grocery store. Opinions were divided. The paper advocates pointed out that paper came from trees, which could be replanted. The plastic advocates argued that many plastic bags were made of recycled materials and could be reused easily. When the teacher checked the answer on the web site quiz, the winner was . . . PLASTIC! The paper advocates were crushed.

But the lesson was not over. The teacher pointed out that the web site had been created by a chemical company that manufactured—you guessed it—plastic! What if the web site had been sponsored by a paper mill? The "correct" solution might have been paper bags!

This story illustrates an important lesson. **You and your students must learn to evaluate information on the Internet.** Just as you evaluate information you read, hear, or see on TV, in magazines, or newspapers, web site evaluation should be an ongoing process.

Answer the following questions before you use a web site in your classroom:
- Who created the web page?
- Does the site include an e-mail address or other way to contact the author?
- When was the page created or updated?
- Is the site trying to sell or promote anything?
- Can I verify information using other sources?

Web site evaluation also deals with utility: how useful is a particular web page in the classroom?
- Does the web page load quickly?
- Is text easy to read?
- Are pictures interesting and grade level appropriate?
- Is the web page easy to navigate?
- Do the links work properly?

It is important to teach young students how to judge the value of what they see. Select several criteria from the lists above and use them as a basis for classroom discussions.

Helpful Hint

Remind students never to give out personal information over the Internet!

Caution!

Grappling with Graphics

Learning to **save and place graphics** (also called images or pictures) is worth the effort. Like text, most Internet graphics can be placed into a word processing or drawing program.

To save graphics:
- Go to the page containing the desired graphics.
- Bookmark the page so you can easily find the graphic again should something go wrong.
- Place the cursor on the graphic.
- Hold down the mouse button.

For Macintoshes:
- Click on a picture, then hold down the mouse button until you see a window.
- Slide down to the **Download Image to Disk** or **Save Image** command. Release the mouse button.

For PCs:
- Hold down the right mouse button until you see a window.
- Slide down to the **Save Image As** command and release the mouse button.

After saving the image:
- Another window will pop up on screen, giving you a choice of where to save the image and what to name it. Name the image and save it to the **desktop** so that it will be easy to find.

To place graphics:
- Open a word processing or drawing program
- Go to the Edit menu
- Use the Paste command to place the picture in the document

Caution!

Use Internet graphics for educational purposes only. When copying text or graphics, it's better to be safe than sorry. Current copyright laws contain a "fair use" policy that allows people to copy some text and graphics for personal, nonprofit, or educational purposes, but reproducing copyrighted text or graphics without permission could land even a well-meaning person in hot water. Look for copyright (©) or trademark (™) symbol identifiers.

Helpful Hint

When you are placing graphics in any program, check to see that the text tool is not selected. If the text tool is selected instead of the pointer tool, the graphic may place as a text element, which can cause your documents not to print.

Hands On

Use the **Saving and Printing Graphics** teacher worksheet (page 27) or the **Printing** student worksheets (pages 47-51) to practice capturing graphics. Use the **Citing Web Sites** sheet (page 18) to find information about citing Internet web sites.

Capture Your Screen

Sometimes a graphic will not allow you to use a pull down menu, even when you click on it. In that case, you can use a procedure known as screen capturing. This skill is too advanced for most young students, but it is a useful skill for teachers. **A screen capture takes a snapshot picture of your entire computer screen.**

Capturing a screen works differently on a Macintosh and a PC, so the directions for both are included here:

For Macintoshes:
- Hold down three keys—Shift, Command, and 3. You may hear a sound like a camera clicking. This places a picture of your screen onto your hard drive. Pictures will be titled Picture 1, Picture 2, etc., in the order in which they are taken.
- Click on your hard drive icon and open the "picture" you just took. The most recent picture will have the highest number. You can now print or add to your picture. You can also copy parts of your picture and paste them into other documents.
- Use the mouse to draw (click and drag) a box around the part of the picture you want to use.
- Go to the Edit menu and select Copy. A copy of your graphic will be placed on the clipboard.
- Open the document where you want to place the image. Select Paste from the Edit menu.

For PCs:
- Use the Print Screen key to make a copy of your screen. This copy is placed on the clipboard; it does not send your picture to the printer.
- If just the Print Screen key does not work, try holding down the Print Screen plus Shift or Print Screen plus Alt keys to place a copy on your clipboard.
- Open the document where you want to place the image. Use the Edit menu to Paste.

Hands On

Practice screen captures using the **Screen Captures for Teachers** worksheet (page 28).

Citing Web Sites

An important part of developing research skills is teaching students to give credit where credit is due. Students cannot copy directly from encyclopedias or other books without citing their sources. Printing information directly from the Internet and including it in a finished report is plagiarism unless the original work is cited. Students who are old enough to do research need to cite their on-line sources, just as they cite other reference materials. Both text and graphics should be documented.

Encourage students to take notes and keep track of sites they visit. Bookmarking locations will help, because it is easy to forget how you arrived at a particular web site. However, if a class is using one computer to research a variety of topics, bookmarks become too numerous. The solution? Write down the location with an old fashioned pencil and paper!

How do you cite a web site? It can be tricky. It is not always possible to tell who authored a page. Web sites change locations and sometimes disappear altogether. Some web addresses are very long and contain many strange symbols.

Proper citation of web sites is an evolving process. Check with your media specialist or search the Internet for the latest developments. However, these citation techniques are designed for adults and can be confusing to younger students who are just learning bibliographic skills.

Below is a sample citation. You may wish to use and teach a slightly different format, depending on which style manual you are accustomed to using. When teaching citation to children, keep it simple, and make sure they understand the principles behind citation. Teach students to look for four items:
• The title of the page
• The author or sponsor. The author may or may not be listed on the web site, but usually is. The web site's sponsor should be readily apparent, as should the type of web site.
• The web address (do not write down the part of the address that comes after the domain)
• The date the web site was last updated. Some web sites, such as weather and news sites, are updated on a daily basis, while others are completed and then never changed again.

Fenix, Jim. National Weather Service, National Oceanic Atmospheric Association. Home page. November 30, 2000. http://www.nws.noaa.gov.

If any of the above information is missing and you and your students have checked carefully, use your best judgment and help your students use theirs. Web sites often are left incomplete or inaccurate, while others are posted quickly without regard to giving credit where credit is due. Fortunately, most of the web sites you and your students will enjoy most are well-maintained and all of the necessary elements for citations are clearly marked.

Caution!

Be aware that there are web sites that provide students with "finished" reports on just about every topic imaginable. Web savvy kids may consider taking advantage of these services. Having students cite their sources will help you determine that their projects are original.

FAQs

What's an FAQ?
FAQ stands for Frequently Asked Question. Many Internet sites have FAQ sections to answer common problems or concerns. The FAQ section of this book is divided into three sections: Classroom Management, Technology Glitches, and Internet Know-how.

Classroom Management

What do I do with students whose parents do not permit them to use the Internet in class?
Students whose parents deny permission should absolutely not be allowed on the Internet. Ask parents if their children can practice off-line computer skills. Involve these students in related projects. For example, have them research more traditional sources, such as encyclopedias or atlases, and compare the results with the Internet research their classmates are completing.

How can I conduct Internet projects with only one computer in my classroom?
To cut down on overcrowded surfing conditions, tailor the assignments in this book to your situation, and include seat work in your lesson plans. Rotate students or groups of students, and schedule specific computer times. Alternately, make a checklist and have each student check off his or her name when the assignment is complete. If you have parent volunteers or teacher assistants, have them work with small groups while other students use the computer.

What can I do if my students play games or read advertisements on the Internet?
Discourage gaming by addressing the problem in the **Classroom Promise** (page 58) your students help construct. Teach students to ignore advertisements. As a last resort, replace a consumer-oriented student with a classmate who is ready to do serious research.

How can I assure parents that their children will be safe on the Internet?
Reassure parents of their children's online safety by keeping the lines of communication open. Make parents aware of your policies and get their permission before beginning Internet projects. Enforce the **Internet Safety Policy** (page 57). Share web sites with parents using the **Places We Have Been!** worksheet (page 59).

What do I do if a student does find inappropriate material on the Internet?
Using kid-friendly search engines should filter out inappropriate material, so do not hesitate to notify the company that produces the web site. Address this issue when writing the **Our Classroom Promise** worksheet (page 58) with your students. Involve parents immediately by sending a note home, and if possible, following up with a meeting or telephone call, depending on the nature of the material. If a child deliberately seeks out inappropriate material, he or she should receive a warning the first time. A second offense should result in suspension of all Internet activity. Some offenses are more serious than others, so you and the child's parents may decide on different levels of discipline.

FAQs

Technology Glitches

Why do some web sites load more slowly than others?

Many factors can influence how quickly web site images appear on your screen. Web sites that are mostly text load fairly quickly. Sites with large color graphics and sound take longer to load because pictures and sound use substantial amounts of memory. Heavy traffic on the Internet can also cause computers to lag. If many people are trying to reach a web site at the same time, it will load more slowly. If a page is taking too long to load, press the Stop button.

My mouse won't move across the screen. What do I do?

If your mouse is moving and your arrow is not, this means your computer may be **frozen**, but check some other potential problems first. Are all your computer cable connections secure? Some may become loose over time just from moving the computer slightly. Try quitting the software you are using. If nothing else works, restart your computer. **On a PC**, press the Control, Alt, and Delete keys twice. **On a Mac**, press the Option, Apple and Esc keys at the same time. Turn off your computer as a last resort only!

What if I get a "not enough memory" message?

A "Not Enough Memory" message means the computer is using too much of its Random Access Memory (RAM). Think of the RAM as the memory your computer is using to make everything run while you sit at the keyboard. If this memory is full, the computer can not operate efficiently. It is the equivalent of trying to have a parent conference, maintain order in your classroom, and plan your next social studies unit all at once. For most computers, additional RAM can be purchased and installed. It's a good investment—the more RAM your computer has, the faster it works.

What do the messages "404 not found" and "connection refused by host" mean?

These and other messages may pop up on your screen, indicating that there is a problem preventing you from accessing a web site. If you typed in a URL, there could be an error in the address. Retype the URL and try again. Alternately, the web site could be busy—try again later. If you continue to get the same response, the web site may have moved or no longer be in existence. Once on a site, you may also get a message which starts with "JavaScript error" or "VBScript error." These are errors in programming language. They may or may not affect whether the web site is working, but can be annoying because they will pop up each time you open that web site.

FAQs

Internet Know-how

What happens if I forget my password?
For password help, contact your school's technology specialist or your ISP. They can't tell you what your password is, but they can delete your old password and allow you to enter a new one.

What's e-mail, and isn't it part of the Internet?
E-mail is short for electronic mail. E-mail is sent via the Internet. Most Internet service providers offer this service. You can also get e-mail through separate software packages or some search engines. An e-mail address, like a URL, contains the @ symbol. The address looks something like: superman@krypton.edu. Your ISP or an independent web site will help you set up an account.

What does it mean to "chat" or visit a "chat room"?
Chat is just what it sounds like—people talking (really, typing) to one another on the Internet. Be careful in chat rooms, especially with younger children. With many chat rooms, you don't know if the person on the other end of the keyboard is an eager student or a convicted felon, so set up chat sessions through a reliable source. For example, another teacher may be willing to try a chat session with your class, or you may have a computer literate parent who could do a live chat as part of a school career day. Some ISPs allow you to create a "buddy list" of chat partners. Make sure you allow only people you know to be on a buddy list. Finally, warn students not to give out **any** personal information, such as last names, addresses, phone numbers, etc.

How can I create my own web page?
Creating a web page is easier now that you no longer have to know a computer programming language called HTML to create web sites. Easy-to-use software programs can help you build web pages. Find a hands-on workshop if you are serious about making a web page (check with your local computer store or school technology expert). Internet service providers will help too, but they may charge a fee to post your site. Fortunately, there are ISPs that offer free web pages to educators, and increasingly, schools are creating and posting their own web pages.

Where can I get help with my computer or with Internet problems?
If your school does not provide a technology specialist to help you with classroom issues, look to a technologically literate faculty member, a parent volunteer, or even a student. Use the help options provided with your software. Many ISPs offer free help by phone, but be prepared for long waits. No matter where you get help, you need to know some basic facts. Refer to the **Internet Data Sheet** (page 60) for a comprehensive list of information you should have handy before calling or asking for assistance.

How to Use These Worksheets

On the following pages are teacher and student worksheets. The student worksheets teach how to use the Internet to do research and have fun. The teacher worksheets are designed to help you, the teacher, become comfortable with the Internet before teaching it to your students, to help you prepare for the students' lessons, and provide you with useful teaching resources. After completing the teacher worksheets, we also recommend that you complete the student worksheets before giving them to your students.

Student worksheets are organized by skill and are designed to be used with the programmable *How To* reference pages. These reference pages provide step-by-step directions and can be posted beside each computer. For example, if you want students to complete the **Happy Holidays** worksheet (page 31), note the skill at the bottom of the worksheet (hyperlinks), and pair the worksheet with the corresponding reference sheet. Next, customize the reference sheet for each specific worksheet activity you want students to complete (see page 23 for instructions). You may want to laminate and display a reference sheet at each computer, or give each student a copy.

- Programmable *How To* reference page

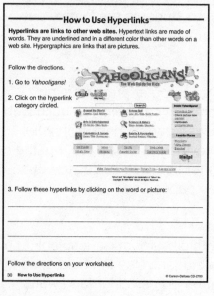

- The **On Your Own** and **With the Class** extensions are optional activities related to the topic students are learning about on the Internet ➡

- Student Worksheet (copy one for each child)

Match the Skill

 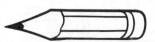

How to Use These Worksheets

Follow the directions below for programming the Reference Pages. The **How to Print** and **How to Set Bookmarks** reference pages do not need to be programmed.

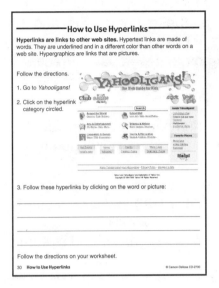 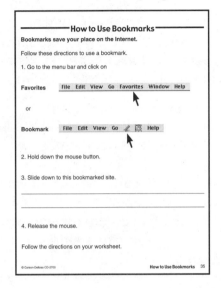 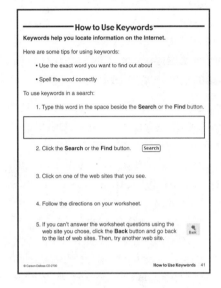

How to Use Hyperlinks
- Use with worksheets on pages 31-34.
- Circle the category in *Yahooligans!* students should click on.
- Write the remaining hyperlinks students should use to get to web sites that will help them finish the worksheets.

How to Use Bookmarks
- Use with worksheets on pages 36-40.
- Set a bookmark on a web site that will provide answers for the worksheets. (See *Bookmarks for Teachers* on page 25 if you need help.)
- Write the name of the bookmark on the line in the pull-down menu.

How to Use Keywords
- Use with worksheets on pages 42-46.
- Fill in the appropriate keyword for each student worksheet:
- page 42 Dinosaurs
- page 43 Penguins
- page 44 Rainbows
- page 45 Ladybugs
- page 46 Whales

- Use with worksheets on pages 48-51.

- Use with worksheets on pages 53-54.

Some web sites may require advanced reading proficiency. Pair pre-readers and beginning readers with an adult or older child.

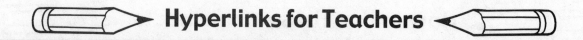

Hyperlinks are text or graphics that represent electronic pathways to other web sites. **Hypertext** is usually underlined and in a different color than surrounding text. **Hypergraphics** vary in appearance, but are identifiable in the same way as hypertext. When in contact with hyperlinks, the arrow cursor will change into a pointing hand. To follow the hyperlink, click on the text or graphic and the new site will appear on your screen. To avoid wasting time bouncing between sites, get all the information you need from your current web location before zooming off to hyperspace. Practice using hyperlinks by filling in the chart below.

- Go to the *Yahooligans!* web site (www.Yahooligans.com).
- Identify the major hyperlink categories. Some are listed in the left column in the chart below.
- Take notes in the right column that will help you remember what you find at each link and how it may be helpful to your students.
- Follow hyperlinks to new sites and examine any hyperlinks you find there.
- To return to a previous page, click the Back button on the tool bar. Make sure you click on the Stop button or allow a page to finish loading before moving on to a new hyperlink.
- Continue the evaluation process, paying attention to the ways hyperlinks organize and streamline the information gathering process.

Name of Hyperlink	What You Can Find There
Around the World	
Arts and Entertainment	
Computers and Games	
School Bell	
Science and Nature	
Sports and Recreation	
Teaching Guide	

Bookmarks for Teachers

Bookmarks are a quick, visible reminder of where you have been on the Internet. They eliminate the need to remember and retype complicated URLs. Use bookmarks to recall web sites you visit regularly or would like to find again. Bookmarks accumulate quickly, so use your Bookmarks menu to organize bookmarks into folders.

To bookmark a page:
- Have the page you want to bookmark on screen.
- On the tool bar, select Favorites or Bookmark.
- Slide down to the "add to . . ." option.
- Release the mouse.

To visit a marked screen:
- Go to the tool bar.
- Select Favorites or Bookmark.
- Slide down to the screen you want to see.
- Release the mouse.

Use this worksheet to plan Internet lessons by finding and bookmarking web sites you will have your students visit, and web sites you will use in your own research and planning. Write each web site's URL in the left column below, and describe the bookmarked web site in the corresponding space to the right. Use this list as a lesson-planning aid and backup, for example, if you or your students accidentally delete your bookmarks.

Name of Bookmark and URL	Site Description
Yahooligans! www.yahooligans.com	A safe, kid-friendly search engine with links to age-appropriate web sites
National Weather Service www.nws.noaa.gov	Government-sponsored weather forecasting and informational web site

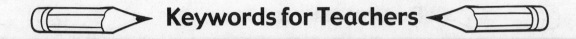# Keywords for Teachers

Getting connected to the Internet is one thing; learning how to navigate this vast information network is quite another. Using **keywords** effectively will make your information gathering expeditions quicker and easier. Experience and practice are the best teachers when it comes to using keywords, so familiarize yourself with these techniques and don't be discouraged if it takes time for your initial searches to yield the results you want. Also, know that keyword searches will yield different results on different search engines. You may find 20 sites for your keyword using one search engine, but only five on another. Refer to the **Keys to the Kingdom** worksheet (page 12) for more information about using keyword qualifiers and eliminators to expand or focus your searches. Use the chart below to practice keyword searches.

• Type in the sample keywords on the left, and explore several URLs that result from these searches in the column to the right.
• Try some of your own keywords to find professional resources on topics which interest you, and add these to the chart.

Keyword	Search Results
lesson plans	
character education	
teaching (teachers)	

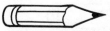 # Saving and Printing Graphics for Teachers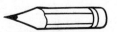

Internet graphics are a wonderful way to liven up written materials. You can add illustrations to worksheets, memos, and letters to parents; give personality to bulletin boards and newsletters; liven up transparencies and folders—anything you can imagine!

Once you know how to copy or save and place graphics, you can add them to almost anything (as long as you respect copyright laws). Go to a web site and find a graphic you want to use.

For Macs:
- Place your cursor on the picture.
- Hold down the mouse button.
- When the menu pops up, slide to the Download Image to Disk command.
- Another screen will pop up, allowing you to save the image to a chosen place on your computer. Saving to the desktop makes it easy to find again.
- The image will have its own name followed by **.gif**, unless you rename it.

For PCs:
- Place your cursor on the picture.
- Hold down the right mouse button.
- Slide to the Save Image As command.
- Release the mouse button.
- Another screen will pop up, allowing you to save the image to a chosen place on your computer. Saving to the desktop makes it easy to find again.
- The image will have its own name followed by **.gif**, unless you rename it.

To place a graphic:
When you have saved all the graphics you need, close your Internet connection. Open the word processing or drawing program where you want to place the graphic.
• Use the particular graphic *place* command your word or graphic program requires to place a graphic.
• Place the picture in your word processing or drawing program.
• Print out your finished product.

- -

Just for Fun
With this scavenger hunt, you can practice copying graphics and find some helpful "teacher stuff" at the same time! Only use images that are cleared for educational use and distribution so that you do not violate any copyright laws (refer to page 18).

1. Find a great apple image to put on a teacher memo! URL: _____

2. Find a cartoon star to put on a "You're a Super Star" certificate!

   URL: _____

3. Copy a computer graphic to add to parent notes or "home made" computer worksheets.

   URL:_____

4. If you are having an open house soon, find a school building to highlight your invitation.

   URL:_____

5. If you have a class pet, copy a graphic of that pet to add to a care instruction sheet.

   URL: _____

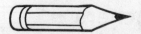 

Screen captures are helpful if you want to show an entire web page. It is useful if you cannot get a graphic to print, because you can copy the entire page, place it, and crop it down to the image you want. You can also crop the image in a drawing program, save it under a different name, then place it into a document. Screen captures, also called screen shots, are useful when used to prepare a class for what the Internet will look like, as in the exercise below.

On a Macintosh:

- Hold down three keys—Shift, Command, and 3. You may hear a sound like a camera clicking. This places a picture of your screen onto your hard drive. Screen shots will be titled Picture 1, Picture 2, etc., in the order in which they are taken.

- Open the document where you want to place the image.

- Use the Edit menu to Paste.

- You can crop parts of the image by drawing a circle around a part of the image, cutting it by using the command under the edit menu, and then pasting it into the document.

On a PC:

- On the keyboard, press the Print Screen key to make a copy of your screen. This copy is placed on the clipboard—it does not send your picture to the printer.

- Open the document where you want to place the image.

- Select Paste under the Edit menu.

- Paste each screen shot into a document each time you take one, because the computer deletes the old one from the clipboard. You cannot save your images unless they are placed into a drawing or word processing program.

Making a Worksheet:

Because it has worked so well for us, we have used the *Yahooligans!* web site to launch most of worksheet exercises. You can familiarize students with this site before they get on the Internet. Following the directions above, capture the *Yahooligans!* screen. Paste it into a document. Copy the directions below onto the document, and allow the students to practice before they start pointing and clicking! You can even capture the home page of a search engine, and let children compare it to another search engine as they use it to complete the exercises. Read the following directions aloud to your young students step by step.

Class Directions

Yahooligans! is a search engine that we will use often in our class Internet exercises. Follow the directions below to answer the questions.

1. Draw a small oval around the words *Language Arts*.

2. Place an X on the search button.

3. Draw a square around the place you can click to get help.

4. Underline the picture that shows where you can find a funny joke.

5. Draw a wavy line through the picture and words that would give you information about your favorite sport.

Name _____

Pointer Practice

Weather
_____

Sports
_____

News
_____

Cut out the hand and arrow pointers. Glue the correct pointer on the screen above to show how to:

1. Scroll down the page.
2. Click on the soccer ball.
3. Click on the word **News**.
4. Scroll up the page.
5. Click on the word that would link to a weather report.

How to Use Hyperlinks

Hyperlinks are links to other web sites. Hypertext links are made of words. They are underlined and in a different color than other words on a web site. Hypergraphics are links that are pictures.

Follow the directions.

1. Go to *Yahooligans!*

2. Click on the hyperlink category circled.

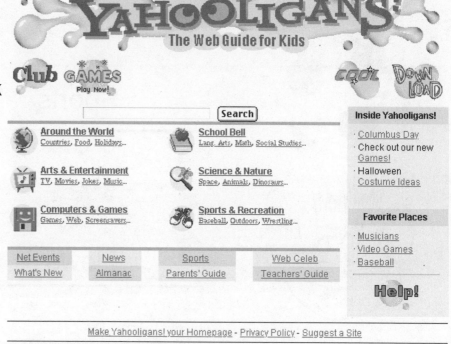

3. Follow these hyperlinks by clicking on the word or picture:

_____

_____

_____

_____

Follow the directions on your worksheet.

Name _____

Happy Holidays

Follow the directions on the How to Use Hyperlinks sheet. Click on the holiday you want to learn about. Answer the questions below.

1. The holiday I chose is _____.

2. The date of this holiday is _____.

3. In the box below, draw things you might see on this holiday.

On Your Own
Make a greeting card for the holiday you chose.

Name _____

Magic

Follow the directions on the How to Use Hyperlinks sheet. Answer the questions below.

1. Find the name of a famous magician. _____

_____

2. Find a magic trick to learn. What is the name of your trick? _____

_____

3. Do your trick for a friend. Did it work? _____

4. Do you believe in magic? Why or why not? _____

_____

5. In the box below, draw a picture of yourself doing your magic trick.

With the Class

Put on a magic show for another class.

Name _____

Pets

Follow the directions on the How to Use Hyperlinks sheet. Find a pet you would like to have. Answer the questions below.

1. The pet I chose is _____.

2. Name your pet _____.

3. How do you care for this pet? _____

_____

_____

4. In the box below, draw a picture of yourself taking care of your pet.

On Your Own
Make a pet care guide for people who own this pet.

Name _____

Music

Follow the directions on the How to Use Hyperlinks sheet. Answer the questions below.

1. Write the instrument names from the word list in the correct box.

Word List			
cello	clarinet	drums	flute
trombone	trumpet	violin	xylophone

Brass	Strings

Percussion	Woodwinds

2. What is your favorite kind of music? _____

On Your Own

Find music on the Internet. Listen to it and draw a picture of what you think of when you hear it. Can you identify any instruments you hear?

How to Use Teacher Bookmarks

Bookmarks save your place on the Internet.

Follow these directions to use a bookmark.

1. Go to the menu bar and click on

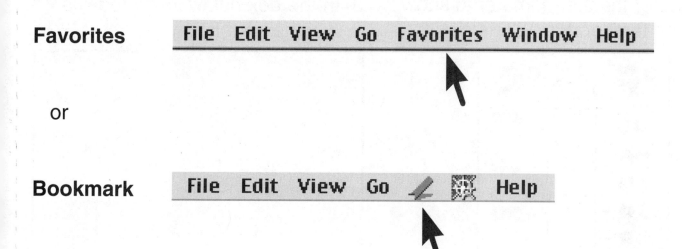

Favorites

or

Bookmark

2. Hold down the mouse button.

3. Slide down to this bookmarked site.

_____

_____

4. Release the mouse.

Follow the directions on your worksheet.

Name _____

Weather

Follow the directions on the How to Use Teacher Bookmarks sheet. Go to the page your teacher has bookmarked about weather. Find out today's weather in another city. Answer the questions below.

1. The city I chose is _____ .

2. Color the thermometer to show the temperature in this city.

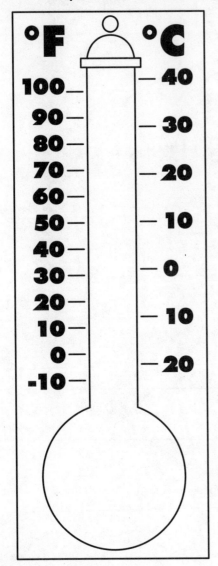

3. In the box below, draw today's weather in this city.

4. In the box below, draw a picture of tomorrow's weather in this city.

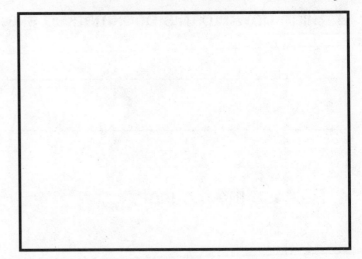

On Your Own
Compare the weather in the city you chose with the weather in your city.

Name _____

Butterflies

Follow the directions on the How to Use Teacher Bookmarks sheet. Use the words in the box to label the pictures of the butterfly life cycle.

adult
caterpillar
chrysalis
egg

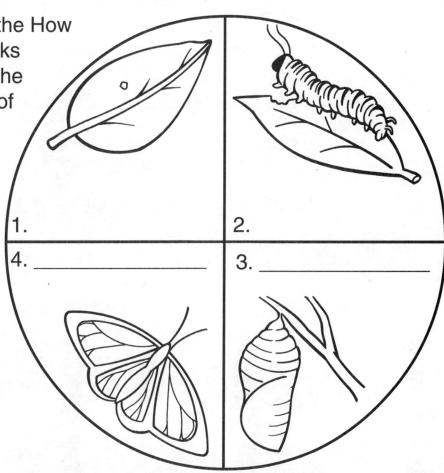

1. _____

2. _____

4. _____

3. _____

Color the butterfly below like one you saw on the Internet. What kind is it?

_____

With the Class

With your classmates, make a mobile using all of your butterflies.

Name _____

Crayons

Follow the directions on the How to Use Teacher Bookmarks sheet to get to a web site about crayons. Answer the questions below.

1. What are the two most popular crayon colors? _____

_____

2. Crayons are made of what two things? _____

_____

3. Color each crayon below the correct color.

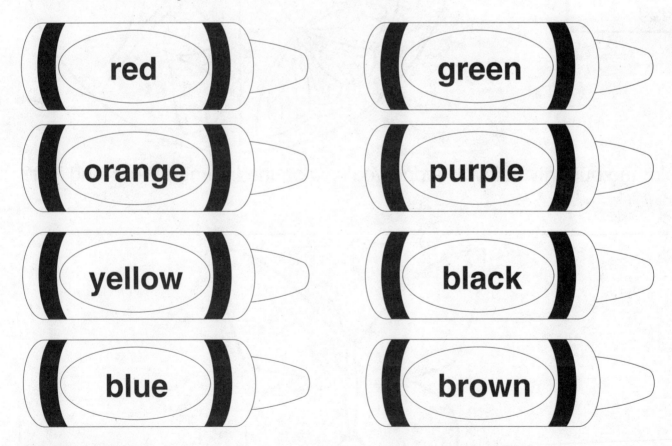

On Your Own
Make a colors booklet. On each page, color a picture of something that is a different color.

Name _____

═══════ **States** ═══════

Choose a state to learn more about. Follow the directions on the How to Use Teacher Bookmarks sheet. Answer the questions below.

1. Which state did you choose? _____

2. What is the state bird? _____

3. What is the state flower? _____

4. What is the state nickname? _____

5. In the box below, draw and color a picture of the state flag.

[ ]

On Your Own

Do any other states touch this state? If yes, write the names of the states.

Name _____

The Moon

Follow the directions on the How to Use Teacher Bookmarks sheet.
Answer the questions below.

1. Color the four phases of the moon.

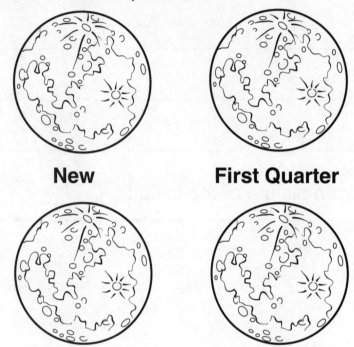

New   **First Quarter**

Full   **Last Quarter**

2. What phase is the moon in today? Color today's moon.

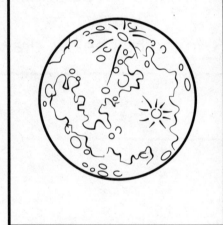

3. Find a moon weight calculator on the Internet.

What is your weight? _____

What is your weight on the moon? _____

Circle the correct answer to finish the sentence below.

4. The moon is a   comet   planet   satellite

On Your Own

There are 28 days between full moons. Find the last full moon. Use a
calendar to count the days until the next full moon.

How to Use Keywords

Keywords help you locate information on the Internet.

Here are some tips for using keywords:

- Use the exact word you want to find out about

- Spell the word correctly

To use keywords in a search:

1. Type this word in the space beside the **Search** or the **Find** button.

2. Click the **Search** or the **Find** button. [Search]

3. Click on one of the web sites that you see.

4. Follow the directions on your worksheet.

5. If you cannot answer the worksheet questions using the web site you chose, click the **Back** button and go back to the list of web sites. Then, try another web site.

Name _____

Dinosaurs

Follow the directions on the How to Use Keywords sheet. Choose a dinosaur to learn about. Answer the questions below.

1. The dinosaur I chose is _____.

2. This dinosaur eats _____.

3. Circle the answer to complete the sentence below.

   This dinosaur could   walk   swim   fly   crawl

4. In the box below, draw and color a picture of your dinosaur.

With the Class

Make a Venn diagram. As a class, divide your dinosaurs into meat-eating or plant-eating dinosaurs (or dinosaurs that eat both).

Name _____

Penguins

Follow the directions on the How to Use Keywords sheet. Answer the questions below.

1. What do penguins eat? _____

2. Baby penguins are called _____.

Circle the correct answer to finish the sentences below.

3. Penguins are   mammals   birds   reptiles

4. Penguins cannot   walk   swim   fly

5. Find the largest type of penguin. Draw a picture of it in the box below.

On Your Own
Write a list of other birds that cannot fly.

Name _____

Rainbows

Follow the direction on the How to Use Keywords sheet. Answer the questions below.

1. What colors are in a rainbow? _____

_____

_____

2. What two things are needed to make a rainbow? _____

_____

3. In the box below, draw your own picture of a rainbow.

On Your Own
Using the first letter of each color, write a funny sentence to help you remember the colors of the rainbow.

Name _____

Ladybugs

Follow the directions on the How to Use Keywords sheet. Answer the questions below.

1. What is another name for a ladybug? _____

2. How many legs does a ladybug have? _____

3. What do ladybugs eat? _____

4. In the box below, draw a ladybug. Color your ladybug. How many spots

   does your ladybug have? _____

On Your Own
Use a paper plate and red and black crayons to make a ladybug. Write ladybug facts on the back of the plate.

Name _____

Whales Scavenger Hunt

Follow the directions on the How to Use Keywords sheet. Answer the questions below.

1. Which whale is white? _____

_____

2. Which whale has a long tooth? _____

_____

3. Which whale is black and white? _____

_____

4. What is a group of whales called? _____

_____

5. What is a baby whale called? _____

_____

6. What is a whale's tail called? _____

_____

7. What does a whale use to breathe? _____

_____

On Your Own
Draw a picture of your favorite whale. On your picture, write one of the facts you learned about whales.

How to Print

The Internet can be a great place to find pictures to print. You can add printed pictures to art projects and reports. Follow the directions below to print pictures from the Internet.

1. Go to the tool bar.

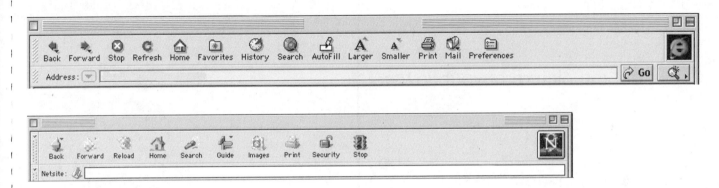

2. Click the **Print** button.

3. A print menu will appear.

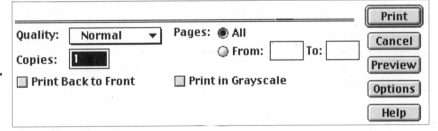

4. Click **Print**.

If your picture does not print, tell your teacher.

Do not try to print again. You could print too many copies!

Be patient! It can take a long time to print a page.

Follow the directions on your worksheet.

Name _____

Flowers

Type in the keyword **flowers**. Find a picture of a flower. Follow the directions on the How to Print sheet to print a picture of your flower. Follow the directions below.

1. Color the picture of your flower.

2. Cut out the picture of your flower.

3. Glue your flower in the box.

4. Use the words below to label the parts of your flower.

leaves	roots
petals	stem

5. If roots, leaves, or stems are not shown on your flower, draw them in and label them.

With the Class

Cut out your picture. Put your pictures together with your classmates' pictures to make a class flower garden.

Name _____

The Zoo

1. Circle a zoo area from the list below.

     African Animals   Aquarium   Bears

     Monkey House   Reptile House   Big Cats

2. Choose an animal you would find in that zoo area. Write the name of the animal you chose.

_____

3. Go to *Yahooligans!* Click on **Animals**, then click on **Zoos**.

4. Find a picture of your zoo animal.

5. Follow the directions on the How to Print sheet to print a picture of your animal.

6. Color the picture of your animal.

7. Cut out the picture of your animal.

With the Class
Draw a class zoo on butcher paper, labeling the zoo areas above. Tape your zoo animal pictures in the correct zoo areas.

Name _____

Coloring Book

Find a page to color on the Internet by following the directions below. Type in the keywords **coloring book**. Look at different web sites and find pictures that you would like to color. Use the How to Print sheet to help you print out your favorite picture. Answer the questions below.

1. What kinds of pictures did you find to color?_____

_____

_____

2. Choose a picture to color. What picture did you choose? _____

_____

_____

3. Why did you choose that picture? _____

_____

_____

4. Think of a title for your picture. _____

_____

5. Color your picture and write your name and the title at the top.

With the Class
Make a frame for your picture. Display all the pictures and create your own art gallery.

Name _____

Printing Scavenger Hunt

Go to *Yahooligans!* Use hyperlinks, keywords, and the How to Print sheet to help you answer the questions below. Be sure to write the names of the web sites where you found your answers.

1. Locate a picture of Smokey Bear. What does Smokey want us to do?

_____

Name of web site _____

2. Look for a picture of Mount Rushmore. Name a president that is carved

into the mountain. _____

_____

Name of web site _____

3. Find a picture that was drawn by Dr. Seuss. Which book by Dr. Seuss

do you think this picture is from? _____

_____

Name of web site _____

4. Locate a picture of a sports ball. What game do you play with it? _____

_____

Name of web site _____

5. Find a picture of the food pyramid. Which food type should you eat

the least? _____

Name of web site _____

How to Set Bookmarks

Bookmarks save your place on the Internet. You can learn to make bookmarks yourself. To make a bookmark, follow the directions below.

1. Go to the page you want to bookmark.

2. Go to the menu bar and click on

Favorites

or

Bookmark

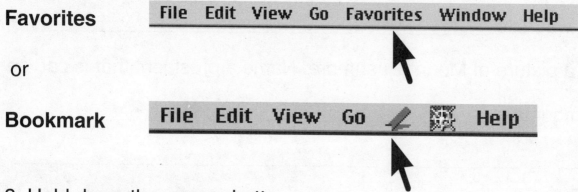

3. Hold down the mouse button.

4. Slide down to the "**Add**" menu.

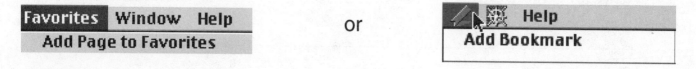

5. Release the mouse.

6. Check to see if your bookmark is on the bookmark list.

7. Write the name of your bookmark below.

Follow the directions on your worksheet.

Name _____

Plants

The study of plants is called botany. Follow the directions to bookmark a web site about plants.

1. Go to *Yahooligans!*

2. Click on **Science**.

3. Click on **Living Things**.

4. Click on **Botany**.

5. Look at different web sites about plants. Choose your favorite web site.

6. Follow the directions on the How to Set Bookmarks sheet to bookmark your favorite web site about plants.

Answer the questions below.

1. My bookmark is called _____.

2. Write a question about plants that can be answered from your

   bookmarked page. _____

   _____

3. Give this page to a friend. See if your friend can open your bookmark and answer your question. Your friend's answer is _____

   _____

On Your Own
Write why you picked this web site to bookmark.

Name _____

Poetry

Follow the directions to bookmark a poem that you like.

1. Go to *Yahooligans!*

2. Click on **School Bell**.

3. Click on **Language Arts**.

4. Click on **Poetry**.

5. Look at different web sites that have poetry.

6. Follow the directions on your How to Set Bookmarks sheet to bookmark your favorite poem.

7. Open three of your classmates' bookmarks and read the poems.

Answer the questions below.

1. Which poem is your favorite? _____

2. Does the poem rhyme?   yes   no

3. Circle the words that best describe the poem.

      funny   sad   scary   exciting

4. Why do you like the poem? _____

_____

On Your Own
Write your own poem and share it with a friend.

Name _____

Internet Scavenger Hunt

Go to *Yahooligans!* Use hyperlinks, keywords, and the How to Print sheet to help you answer the questions below. Be sure to write the names of the web sites where you found your answers.

1. What is the Caldecott medal awarded for? _____

_____

Name of web site _____

2. How many sides does a snowflake have? _____

_____

Name of web site _____

3. What is a baby turkey called? _____

_____

Name of web site _____

4. What is the name of a famous circus? _____

_____

Name of web site _____

Name _____

Internet Scavenger Hunt

5. What is the capital of Japan? _____

_____

Name of web site _____

6. How many legs does a tarantula have? _____

_____

Name of web site _____

7. What is another name for the constellation The Big Dipper? _____

_____

Name of web site _____

8. Who invented the telephone? _____

_____

Name of web site _____

9. How do you say "hello" in the African language Swahili? _____

_____

Name of web site _____

Internet Safety Policy/Approval Form

Dear Parents,

Our class is getting ready to learn how to use the Internet. We have discussed some Internet safety rules and written a Classroom Promise. Familiarize yourself with these guidelines and the Classroom Promise we have developed as a class. Please sign and return the bottom portion of this form to let us know you are familiar with these policies and agree to allow your child to use the Internet in classroom-related activities. Note that before any student can use the Internet in our classroom, he or she must also read and sign the bottom portion of this sheet.

Classroom Internet Safety Policy

1. Students will use the Internet only with permission from the teacher.

2. When students are using the Internet, they cannot give out any personal information, such as names, addresses, telephone numbers, etc.

3. Students will notify a teacher immediately if they see any information that makes them feel uncomfortable.

4. Students must stay in approved, appropriate areas of the Internet.

5. Failure to follow school Internet policies will result in Internet privileges being revoked.

✂--

Classroom Internet Approval Form

Student:_____   Teacher:_____

I have read the classroom promise and the Internet safety policies of our classroom and I agree to follow them. I understand that **not** following these rules means I **cannot** use the Internet at school.

Student's Signature:_____   Date:_____

I have read the classroom promise and the Internet safety policies of the class and agree to allow my child to use the Internet and participate in Internet-related classroom activities.

Parent's Signature:_____   Date:_____

Our Classroom Promise

Our class has talked about Internet safety. We know that there are rules we must follow. We have discussed how to be good citizens in class while using the Internet. Our class promises:

_____

_____

_____

_____

_____

_____

_____

_____

We understand that only students who keep
this promise can use the Internet.

Places We Have Been!

Dear Parents,   Date: _____

Our class has been using the Internet to learn many new and interesting things! We want you to know all the exciting places we have been. If you have access to a computer at home, at the public library, or at a friend's house, you might like to visit these kid-safe Internet sites, too!

We have visited these Internet web sites:	We have been learning about:

✂ --

Parent Internet Feedback Form

We appreciate your comments and feedback! If you have Internet-related knowledge, or know of any kid-safe Internet sites you would like to recommend, please send that information to your child's teacher.

Date: _____

Teacher's Name: _____

Student's Name: _____

Web Site Information or Comments: _____

_____

Internet Data Sheet

This page is designed to help you record important basic information about your computer and your Internet connection. Consult your Owner's Manual and your Internet Service Provider if necessary. Keep this information in a safe place and refer to it as needed. You may need this information when dealing with technical support contacts, network administrators, or when upgrading your current computer system.

Make and Model of Computer (iMac, Power Macintosh 8600, IBM Aptiva E530, etc.):

_____

Amount of RAM (Random Access Memory) Installed in Computer:

_____

Type of Connection Used:

❏ External Modem   Model: _____ Speed: _____

❏ Internal Modem   Model: _____ Speed: _____

❏ Direct Network Connection—No Modem Necessary

Your Internet Service Provider:

_____

Your Internet Service Provider's Web Address:

_____

Your Internet Service Provider's Customer Support Phone Number: _____

Your User Name (Log On ID):

_____

Your E-mail Address:

_____

Remember Your Password—Do Not Write It Here!

Glossary

America Online (AOL) A large, very popular Internet service provider

Acceptable Use Policy (AUP) A set of rules and guidelines which regulate Internet use in a district, school, or classroom

Bookmark The Netscape term for marking an Internet site so you can return to it quickly and easily

Browser A program such as Netscape Navigator or Microsoft Internet Explorer that enables you to navigate the Internet

Chat/Chat Room Real-time, interactive communication between people on the Internet, often centered around a certain topic of conversation

.com A domain name indicating a commercial web site

Cyberspace Name for the worldwide electronic network of computer connections

Desktop The screen you see when your computer first starts up

Domain Name The last group of letters in an Internet address, indicating the nature of the site; for example, .com indicates a commercial site

.edu A domain name indicating an educational web site

e-mail Abbreviation for electronic mail messages sent via the Internet; a service offered by many Internet service providers

Favorites The Internet Explorer term for marking an Internet site so you can return to it quickly and easily

.gov A domain name indicating a U.S. government web site

Home page The first page you see when you log-on to the Internet. Also, the first page which appears for any web site

Glossary

Hyperlinks Direct connections to other sites on the Internet, represented by words, called *hypertext*, or pictures, called *hypergraphics*

Hypertext Markup Language (html) The original computer programming language of the Internet; used to create web pages

Hypertext Transfer Protocol (http) The abbreviation at the beginning of Internet addresses (URLs), which allows computers to read and transfer information to and from different locations on the Internet

Icon A picture or graphic symbol representing a particular computer program or function

Internet An enormous, interconnected network that links millions of computers all over the world

Internet Explorer A major Internet browser; a product of Microsoft

Internet Service Provider (ISP) Any one of a number of companies that provides customers with software and services related to the Internet; for example: America OnLine, CompuServe, Prodigy, and Mindspring

Keywords Words or phrases that guide search engines in looking for information

Log On To get on the Internet by typing your user name and password

.mil A domain name indicating a U. S. military web site

Modem A device that electronically connects your computer to the Internet by translating computer language and then transmitting it over telephone lines

Net A commonly-used abbreviation for Internet

.net A domain name indicating a web site with network resources

Glossary

Netscape Navigator A major Internet browser

Network Any group of computers that have been electronically linked together

.org A domain name indicating a nonprofit organization or agency

Password Words and/or letters that allow access to a computer program or network

Random Access Memory (RAM) Internal memory that holds data and programs currently being executed by the computer

Screen Capture A graphic "snapshot" of your computer screen

Search Engine Any one of many Internet vehicles, such as *Yahooligans!*, which search the web for information using keywords or hyperlinks

Surf Popular term for browsing the Internet; looking at different web sites

Uniform Resource Locator (URL) The unique electronic address of any specific web site

User Name The name you use to identify yourself when logging on to the Internet

Web page One page of any specific location on the Internet

Web site Any specific location on the Internet; usually made up of several web pages

World Wide Web (WWW) The first three letters in web site addresses that are not e-mail addresses.

Yahoo! A popular search engine which provides a kid-safe directory called Yahooligans!

Answer Key

Page 34 Music

- brass: trombone, trumpet
- strings: cello, violin
- percussion: drums, xylophone
- woodwinds: clarinet, flute

Page 37 Butterflies

1. Egg
2. Caterpillar
3. Chrysalis
4. Adult

Page 38 Crayons

1. blue and red
2. paraffin wax and colored pigment

Page 43 Penguins

1. fish, squid, krill
2. chicks
3. birds
4. fly

Page 44 Rainbows

1. Red, Orange, Yellow, Green, Blue, Indigo, Violet
2. Water droplets (rain) and sunlight

Page 45 Ladybugs

1. ladybirds, ladybeetles
2. six
3. aphids

Page 46 Whales Scavenger Hunt

1. Beluga
2. Narwal
3. Orca
4. A pod
5. A calf
6. Fluke
7. Blow hole

Page 51 Printing Scavenger Hunt

1. Prevent forest fires
2. Washington, Lincoln, Jefferson, Roosevelt
3. answers may vary
4. answers may vary
5. fats and sweets

Pages 55–56 Internet Scavenger Hunt

1. children's book illustrations
2. six
3. poult
4. answers may vary
5. Tokyo
6. eight
7. Ursa Major, The Big Bear
8. Alexander Graham Bell
9. hello = jambo